Native American Courting Flute

Easy-to-Follow Flute Instructions

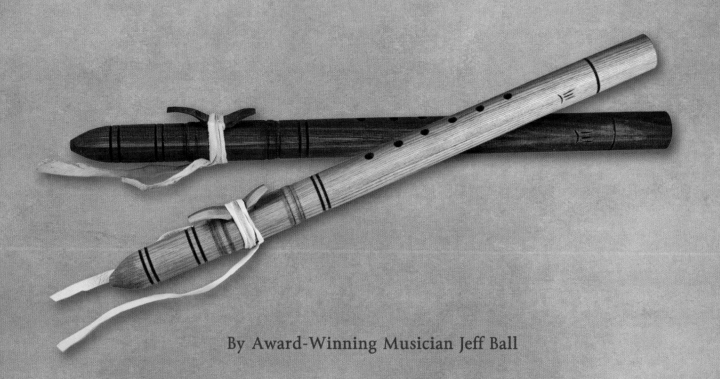

By Award-Winning Musician Jeff Ball

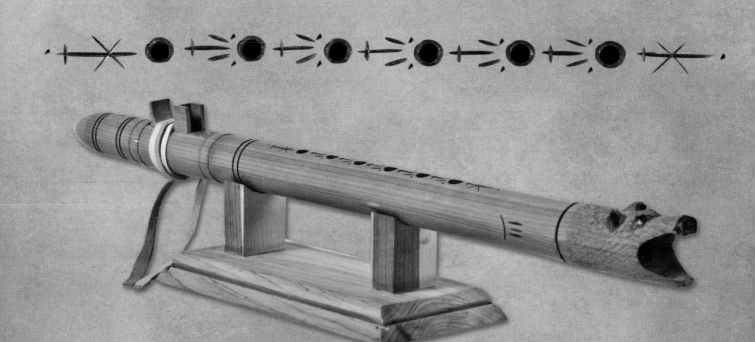

Published by: Crazy Crow Trading Post
1801 Airport Road
Pottsboro, TX 75076
903-786-2287
www.crazycrow.com

(ISBN) 1-929572-22-0

Printed in the U.S.A.

Wordsmith: Jeff Ball
Cover Design: Michael Catellier
Designed: Michael Catellier and J. Rex Reddick
Illustrated: Randall Ball
Photography: Michael Catellier and Jeff Ball
General Support and Encouragement: Margo Boone

Special Thanks

I want to thank everyone who has taken time to further the evolution of this instrument. It has become an important part of my life and provided me with a form of expression that I can't imagine I would have found in any other way. My music and the friendships that have formed as a result are among my most treasured.

Flute player by Barthel "Buddy" Little Chief, Kiowa. Courtesy of the Gray Major Collection.

Painting of a Comanche Flute Player by "Black Moon" (Leonard Riddles), Comanche. Courtesy of the Walter T. Parker Collection.

Table of Contents

Prologue

Several years ago I wrote a book titled *Trailhead of the American Indian Courting Flute*. In the decades that have passed since its release, I've learned a great deal more about this wonderful instrument and have an even better grasp of its capabilities. I've watched as the Native American Flute (NAF) has grown to be far more than just a museum piece or curiosity. The NAF has evolved and become more popular than anyone could have imagined thanks in large part to the Internet.

My journey with the NAF began many years before the Internet when I attended a Powwow in Baltimore, MD. Most of the day I roamed the Powwow grounds looking at the crafts for sale, hearing the drum, and watching the dancers. I enjoyed them all but was most taken when the drums and dancers took a break and the flute player stepped forward. The sound of that flute called to me and I quickly went looking for recordings of flute music. The more I listened to the recordings I bought that day, the more I wanted to try and play one myself. Unfortunately I had two problems standing in my way. The first was where to find a NAF and the other was how I would learn to play…since I had no musical experience. Several months later I had located a flute and was introduced to a Choctaw man named Windtamer who helped me get started.

As time passed I thought having a manual to teach the basic techniques of the flute would have been helpful. I also realized how much more difficult the learning process would have been if it were not for the guidance of Windtamer. It was with these things in mind that I approached longtime friend Bruce Whitten and Trailhead Flutes began. We tried to write a manual for the absolute beginner as well as the seasoned player. I have learned a lot since writing that book and know that you will be a better player because of it.

Introduction

The NAF is one of the oldest instruments in North America. It was originally used for relaxation and as part of the courting ritual. If you spend some time learning the basics you are sure to enjoy playing for many years. This manual and the CD that accompanies it will help you learn the basic skills needed to play your flute. As with all things you will need to practice regularly to develop and refine your skills. When I began I carried my flute everywhere and played as much as possible. Try playing your flute in a stairwell, parking garage, or a squash court. Playing in locations like these will allow you to hear the flute's voice carry. Many recording artists duplicate this effect by playing into a digital delay or using a reverb effect.

When I was learning to play the NAF I listened exclusively to flute music. I'd listen in my car, at home, or head back out to the Powwow to hear more live flute music. This may sound a bit excessive, but without the distractions of other musical influences, all my focus could remain on learning the song of the flute. During this process, the song of the NAF became a natural part of my subconscious…making it that much easier to play without thinking.

I suggest you invest in a few recordings by various artists and listen to each musician's style of play. The tricky part of this approach is to avoid playing like someone else. You want to hear how they arrange their songs, listen to their embellishments, and then find your voice. Your style of play should reflect the music within you, not mimic the songs of another. If you play another person's music…you are playing another person's soul. This is your story, your feelings; these will be your songs.

Mandeh-Kahchu (Eagle's Beak), Mandan - This watercolor was painted by Karl Bodmer, a Swiss artist in the early 1830s and represents one of the earliest examples depicting a Native American flute. From a print in a private collection.

The Legend

Men have always needed other worldly assistance in attracting and keeping the women they loved. Long ago, Indian warriors were shown a secret which helped them win the hearts of these women. This is the story of how the Indian Courting Flute became an integral part of the courting ritual. Many tribes have a legend which tells how the flute came to their tribe. This is one version of that ancient story.

Long ago a great hunter and warrior was enraptured by a chieftain's daughter. Although his bravery and hunting skills were without equal in the eyes of the tribe, he was afraid to express his heart to the one he loved. Instead, he was forced to look on as other warriors more skilled in speaking with women courted his heart's desire.

Knowing the love charm was contained in the elk magic, he set out hunting for a great elk in hopes of capturing both meat for the village and the young girl's heart. Outside the village he found the largest set of elk tracks he had ever seen. Eagerly he set out on the trail, knowing if he could capture the magic of this elk he could easily win the one he loved.

He followed the tracks for three days, catching only brief glimpses of the great elk. The tracks finally lead to a small stream miles from the village and there they stopped. Stunned, he carefully searched the entire area for some sign of where the elk had gone but found nothing. Realizing the sun was low in the sky, and any further attempts to track at this late hour would be futile, he made camp.

As he drifted to sleep with a heavy heart, the night song suddenly changed. Drifting through the blackness was a mournful song he had never heard before. At first the song made him afraid, and he grabbed for his bow. Then as he listened, he felt the song soothe his troubled heart. Weary from his travels he finally slept.

During his slumber, he dreamt of the haunting music flowing through the forest. The image of a woodpecker with a bright red crown filled his dream, seeming to taunt him. *"Follow me,"* it cried. *"Follow me, for I know a secret."*

Upon waking, he heard the song calling from within the forest. He set off to find the song's source for he knew this was why he had been led here.

The song brought him to the edge of a clearing where he saw the woodpecker from his dream perched on the branch of a cedar tree. As he walked toward the tree, the song became stronger. The branch beneath the woodpecker was singing. The branch sang to him with every breath of the wind.

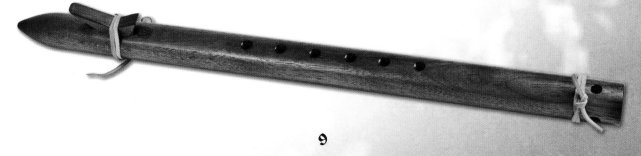

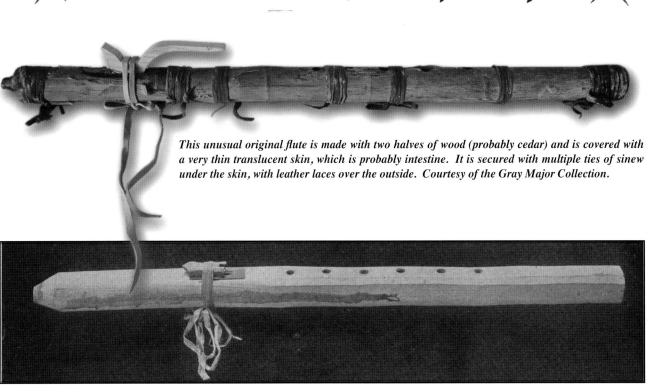

This unusual original flute is made with two halves of wood (probably cedar) and is covered with a very thin translucent skin, which is probably intestine. It is secured with multiple ties of sinew under the skin, with leather laces over the outside. Courtesy of the Gray Major Collection.

"Flageolet (Lover's Flute)" - This photo is Plate 2 from the 1913 Bureau of American Ethnology Bulletin 53, Chippewa Music - II by Frances Densmore.

"Flageolet" - This photo is Plate 5 from the 1922 Bureau of American Ethnology Bulletin 75, Northern Ute Music by Frances Densmore.

The branch had been hollowed by the industrious woodpecker giving the wind a place to sing. The warrior entreated to the woodpecker to let him take the branch back to his village. With the woodpecker's agreement he began his journey home with renewed hope.

As he walked, all the sounds of nature seemed new to him as he thought of how to weave them together into the song that would surely win the young girl's affection.

At the end of the first day of his journey home, he tried to bring the song through the branch... to no avail. He tried waving the branch through the air, but no sound came. He tried blowing across the holes, and again the branch remained silent. Finally, knowing he would not learn the secret on his own, he prayed for wisdom. For three nights he fasted and implored the spirits for guidance.

On the third night of his prayers, the woodpecker returned to his dream and transformed into a man. "Come," he said, "let me show you the secrets of this song." In his vision he watched as the feathered spirit hollowed out a branch of cedar and began to play. Upon walking the young man began to search for a cedar tree that would provide him with the wood for his courting flute. It was to be a special branch for it would sing what he was unable to speak. After finding a branch approximately the length of his arm, and as straight as any arrow, he began to shape the branch as the spirit had shown him. While crafting his flute he visulized the young girl's reaction upon first hearing him speak to her through the flute. As a token of his gratitude, he carved the speaking end of the flute to resemble the woodpecker who had guided him.

After completing his flute, he began his journey home. His heart felt light as he moved among nature's children, blending their voices into his song. With excitement and confidence he went to a hill at the edge of the village. He quieted himself, listened to his heart, and began to play. The wind carried his song into the village where everyone stopped to listen. Anyone who heard the warrior's song felt the love and peace within the flute's song. But it was the chieftain's daughter that this song was meant for, and it touched her deeply. She gatherred a blanket and left her father's tepee to join the warrior on the hill. She listened to him play, stunned that he could convey so much love without speaking a word, and thrilled by the message he was sending. Her heart filled with joy as she realized he was weaving their hearts together through this melody.

To this day, as the day fades into night, you can hear the young warrior's song in the voices of the birds carried on the breath of the wind, within the spirit of the forest.

This Hopi man was photographed between 1880 and 1890 at Mi-shong-na-vi, Arizona. He wears body paint, a kilt, sash, an eagle feather bustle, necklaces, a hair ornament and is carrying an un-usually long flute. Courtesy of Denver Public Library, Denver, Colorado. X-30789

Taken sometime between 1870 and 1880, this Charles A. Zimmer-man photograph shows a young Sioux girl wrapped in a plaid blan-ket and playing the flute. Women did not typically use flutes so this is most likely a "romantic" photograph staged by the photographer with a flute used as a prop. Courtesy of Denver Public Library, Denver, Colorado. X-31764

Left: R. Carlos Nakai, prolific Native American performing and recording artist, educator, and student of the Native American flute. Nakai has become the "linchpin in NAF performance and education".

Above: Identified on this print as Kiowa, this man is playing a wooden flute, with a drum hanging from his arm. This is most likely a staged photo using props from the photographer as the parts of his clothing indicate mixed tribal styles, with Plains style leggings, a Great Lakes area shirt, Prairie style turban and Plateau beaded belt. Circa 1880 - 1910. Courtesy of Denver Public Library, Denver, Colorado. X-32402

Left: Studio portrait of a Ute man playing the flute while seated. He wears a roach with a single eagle feather, hairpipe choker, earrings, commercial shirt and vest, wool leggings, ankle bells and moccasins, and has a Navajo style blanket wrapped around his waist. Interestingly, attached to his vest is a medal reading in part: "Denver". Courtesy of Denver Public Library, Denver, Colorado. X-30370

Modern Native American Flute History

I am not a historian, but I've traveled a lot, I've met many people, and have payed attention. During the early 1900s the NAF basically became a museum piece. A few men across the country were still making and playing the NAF but its voice was heard less and less as the years passed. The tuning of those first flutes was very different from the tuning used today. The original flutes were made according to the dimensions of the flutes maker. The length of the flute was roughly as long as the makers arm. The distance between the sound holes (nest) and the first hole on the fingerboard was about the span of the maker's hand and the spacing of the holes was about that of a thumb.

Dr. Richard Payne is one of two key players in the modern life of the NAF. Doc Payne collected flutes from all over the country and spent time with many of the old style flute players. Doc is also credited with passing a functional NAF along to a few men who would go on to record with the flute and expand it's voice.

Another pivotal figure in the renaissance of the NAF was O.W. Jones. Like Doc, OW studied museum flutes and spoke with old style players. O.W. Jones is credited with giving R.Carlos Nakai his first functional flute. R.Carlos Nakai would go on to become the linchpin in NAF performance and education. Nearly every modern flute player has been influenced by his music and I am of the opinion that his style of play determined what has become Native Flute Music.

The most important figure in NAF construction has to be Michael Graham Allan – a.k.a. Coyote Old Man. Like Doc Payne and O.W. Jones, Michael was interested in the NAF and visiting museum collections around the country. Michael was a fan of the shakuhachi, which had a beautiful scale but was hard to play. He was also interested in the NAF which had no real tuning to speak of so he applied the shak tuning to the NAF which he says was the best of two worlds. A beautiful tuning on an instrument that was easy to play.

When I began playing flute I could only find a few archival recordings and music by John Huling, Kevin Locke, Tom Mauchahty-Ware, R. Carlos Nakai, Doc Tate Nevaquaya, Coyote Old Man, Tsa'ne Dos'e, and John Rainer, Jr. I was part of the second wave of flute players that included Douglas Spotted Eagle, Joseph Firecrow, Charles Littleleaf, Robert Mirabal, Bill Miller, Perry Silverbird, and Mary Youngblood. Bill Miller is a huge name in native music and was actually recording back in the early 1980s…before almost any of us. Although he used the flute in some of his earlier recordings I'm not aware of a solo flute recording prior to 1991.

The New Age movement of the late 80s and early 1990s helped to bolster the resurgence of the flute as nature stores and record shops nationwide started to play and sell Native Flute music. It was after the Internet was commercialized around 1995 that American Indian Flute music, instruments, and teachers were all more accessible and the instruments popularity began to soar.

The Basics

This manual is developed to introduce you to the basics of playing the NAF. The techniques you learn from this manual can be applied to either five or six-hole flutes. I have used a six-hole flute to demonstrate the lessons on the CD.

Before you get started it is important to know the names of the various parts of the flute. Since this text is not intended to teach you how to make a flute I'll use the common names for each part of the flute rather than those used by flute makers.

The block of wood tied to the top of the flute is commonly called a block. It's often carved to look like an animal but may just appear to be a block of wood. The block sits on a flat area and covers two holes in the flute – known as a nest. The first hole, which is closest to your mouth, will be covered by the block. The second hole will be left uncovered by the block. The flute voice will come from this spot on the flute, not at the flutes end.

To hold the flute properly you will use the middle three fingers of each hand. The thumb and pinky help stabilize the flute. My preference is to hold my left hand above the right but the choice is yours. When covering a hole, use the pad of your fingertip rather than the tip of your finger. Covering holes in this way ensures a tight seal resulting in purer notes and fewer squeaky leaks.

When you are ready to play your flute, your lips should be pursed similar to a whistle. Do not wrap your lips around the end of the flute. Most beginners find they are most successful when blowing gently. You can increase the blowing force as you become more accomplished and comfortable with your abilities.

Maintenance of Your Flute

There are three basic ways you can do damage to your flute. The first problem is moisture. Moisture is a constant problem since it can build up beneath the block rather quickly. The quick and easy solution is to remove the block and wipe the area clean. It's not a bad idea to turn the flute upside down and give it a shake too.

Keep an eye on the fingerboard area of your flute since the finish can become worn. This is usualy something that happens when flutes are finished with beeswax rather than the polymers that many of the better flute makers use. I've owned a lot of flutes over the years and very few required any maintenance. I suggest you speak with the person who made your instrument and follow his or her advice.

The second thing you'll need to be aware of is breaking your flute. While the flutes are not necessarily fragile, they definitely fall under the category of "Handle With Care". Most flutes will come with a cloth bag but that's only good for keeping bugs out and minimizing scratches. There are a few companies making cases of various sizes that will get your flute around safely. If you're traveling with several flutes at once I've seen many flute makers use a gun case. They tend to be pretty strong and are usually the right size.

The third threat to your flute comes from dogs. Man's best friend does not see a beautifully handcrafted instrument. Your dog will not appreciate the exotic wood, the ornate detail carved into the block design, nor the tonal quality. Flute = Stick.

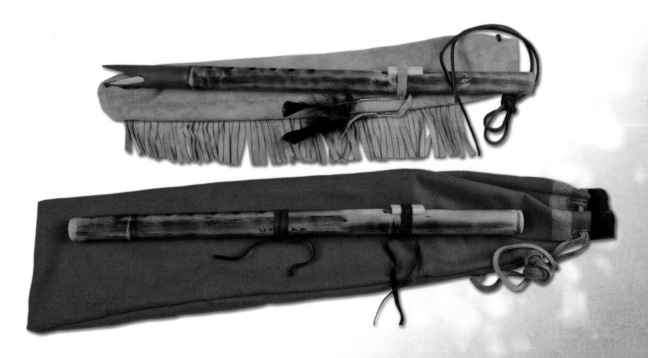

Lesson Key

The hole closest to the bottom of the page is the one closet to your mouth. You are looking down the flute.

Flute with all holes open

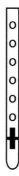

Holes without shading are open. Holes that are shaded are covered with a finger.

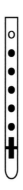

A comma separates multiple steps within an exercise.

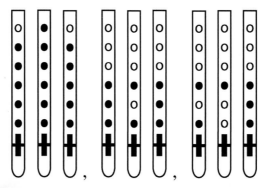

You may find it helpful to listen to the lesson on the CD before attempting the exercise. Hearing the exercise played should help you to get the hang of things more quickly.

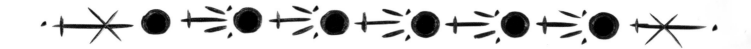

Getting Started

In this lesson your goal is simply to cover the holes without allowing air to escape beneath your fingers. Stand in frond of a mirror and cover the three holes closet to your mouth – leave the bottom three holes open. Blow into the flute and listen for the note to be played cleanly. When I say cleanly - I mean without squeaks - said another way, it's a note you would like to hear.

If you are hearing squeaky notes, adjust your fingers and make certain that all holes have a good seal. Standing in front of a mirror will allow you to locate which finger is not covering a hole more quickly than guessing.

Once you can play a constant and pleasant note with the top three holes covered, try covering the fourth hole with the index finger of your other hand. Repeat the same process for each of the remaining open holes until you are able to play a pleasing note with all holes covered.

Tip: The amount of air pressure you have to use when covering the last hole can be tricky and it varies from flute to flute. It will be easy for you to get this bottom note, or root note, once you've been playing for a while. Covering all the holes well and getting "just the right amount" of air pressure on the root note are the two biggest challenges you'll have to learn to play the NAF. Take your time, practice, and you'll get it rather quickly…it's down hill from here.

Root Over Blow

Once you are comfortable making sound with the flute and are able to play the root note with some control you're ready for the over blow. Not all flutes will over blow, but most will.

Q: "I've never played the NAF so how will I know if my flute doesn't over blow?"

A: If you didn't have any trouble learning to play the root note you're either a gifted player *"or"* your flute won't play the over blow.

Start with all holes covered and play the root note. Gradually increase the amount of air pressure until the note jumps up an octave. Once you can over blow at will, try holding the octave and then reduce the air pressure allowing the root note to return.

The Basic Scale

In this exercise you will learn to play many of the basic notes on your flute. Always be mindful of your air pressure, trying to maintain a constant tone.

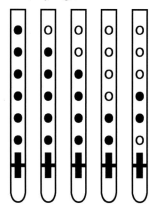

Once you feel comfortable playing the scale forward, try playing it backwards and forwards.

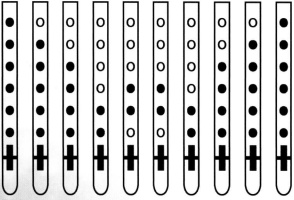

Minor Pentatonic Scale

The minor scale has two more notes than the basic scale. Higher notes like the last two shown may require more air pressure to obtain and the fingering may vary from flute maker to flute maker. Most makers will provide you with a finger chart to show you how their individual flutes will get the notes.

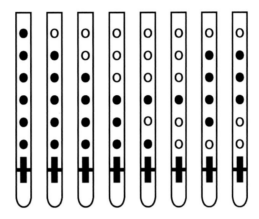

Minor Scale

One of the easiest scales to play is the minor scale. In fact, the only tricky note included is that sweet root note that probably caused you to select your flute in the first place.

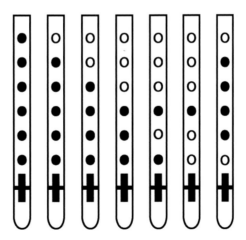

Blues Scale

A slight variation of the minor scale adds just one note but changes the feel of the flute entirely.

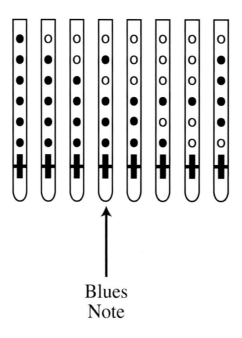

Blues
Note

The Flutter

The fluttering sound, or trill, produced on the CD in lesson 3 is one of the many distinct sounds produced by the NAF. To do this correctly you'll need to lift one or more fingers and replace them several times in quick succession. Begin with holes 1, 2, and 3 covered. Close and open hole 4 three times. Go as fast or slow, as you want. The sound you're trying to make comes from the change on hole #4

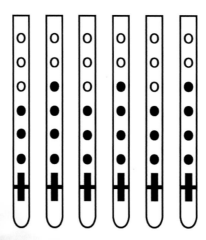

Chirping

Chirping is sometimes called a grace note and is another sound commonly associated with the NAF. This sound can appear anywhere in the song; before a note, after a note, or all by itself…the choice is yours. For minimal contrast in the sound of your chirp, try lifting the finger closet to the next note you intend to play – see lesson 4-A. You can maximize your chirp sound by lifting a finger that is farther away from your endnote. This is demonstrated in lesson 4-B

Position B = Holes 1 and 2 are covered
Positions C, D, and E = the chirp! The quickness of the transition between
positions D and E determine success.

Lesson 4-A

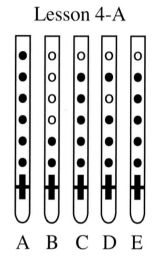

A B C D E

The positions D and E determine success.

Lesson 4-B

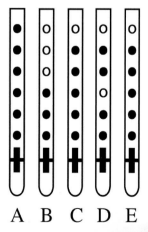

A B C D E

Distinctive Notes

Many times you play notes simply by changing which fingers are raised and lowered. Sometimes you'll want to lead the note off with a more crisp sound. This is accomplished with a flick of the tongue. Simply move your tongue as you would if you were to say a soft "T" (say "tuh"). Now try saying "tuh" as you lead off a note. This technique is known as tonguing and can be heard in lesson 5. Listen to example #5 on your CD and then try it yourself. When you get comfortable with the sound of this technique you can shut the CD off and try it yourself.

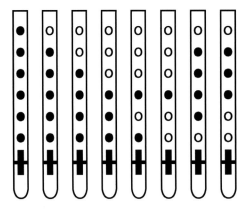

Note Bending

If you listen to enough flute players you'll get used to hearing a lot of hot-handed, fast fingering, which is great, but the magic of this instrument is held in it's ability to express emotion. Note bending is a terrific technique for expressive play. The best part is that it's also an easy technique to learn. When one of the flutes holes is uncovered, slowly roll your finger over the hole. When done at the correct speed and with a slight adjustment to your air pressure, you'll make a smooth transition from one note to the next. The same effect can also be done in reverse by peeling or prying the finger off of a covered hole.

Slowly lower and raise the finger over hole #4.

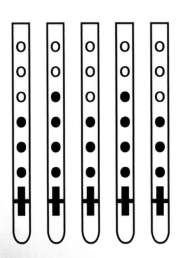

22

Nature Sounds

The NAF can mimic several sounds of nature. One of the more unusual sounds is similar to a frog or cricket. To make this vibrating sound, you can either roll your tongue or adjust the shape of your mouth and make your uvula wiggle (the uvula is the punching bag that hangs from the back of your mouth.) Try to make the sound through your flute.

Another animal sound that the NAF can make is the call of a loon. The loon call is made by covering holes 4 and 5, then blowing into the flute with enough force to produce an octave jump. Breath control is essential to produce the call which best emulates the loon. Gradually increase the force of your breath until the octave jump happens…then, reduce your blowing force, allowing the tone to drop back down.

Modern cedar flute made by Tom Ogletree, Marieitta, GA and beaded by George Gray Major. Courtesy of the Gray Major Collection.

Vibrato

This lesson deals with breath control and will raise your level of play. The sound produced by sending short bursts of air through the flute can be produced two ways.

One option is to inhale deeply and blow several quick puffs of air as though you're blowing out several candles one – at – a – time.

Option two has the puffs coming from your diaphragm. Inhale deeply and then quickly contract your diaphragm as though you're laughing. This technique can be done at anytime during play. The truth is that you'll eventually use both methods without even thinking about it. Try this technique with holes 1, 2, and 3 covered.

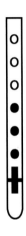

Half Hole Drill

You will have the occasion to play only half of one hole at a time. This is a tricky technique but one that will pay off for you time and again. As with all things, the best way to gain confidence is to practice. You can half-hole any note to expand the range of your flute but I'm going to suggest you practice the major scale first.

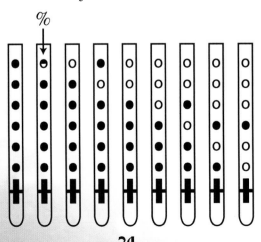

24

Improvisations

I've taught many people to play the NAF over the years and often hear students complain that they just don't know what to play. A simple solution to this problem is playing a melody that you're very familiar with, such as "Happy Birthday". The next step may sound a bit odd but it really works.

Do not worry if the melody you play does not sound like the melody in your head…it shouldn't. Read that again. The melody you play should NOT sound like the melody in your head. You're simply trying to move beyond the writer's block and stumble onto something new. Before you know it, you will be playing a new melody and have something new to work with.

"Flute Player" by Enoch Kelly Haney, Seminole. In addition to being an internationally known Native American artist from Oklahoma, Haney has served as Principal Chief of the Seminole Nation of Oklahoma and was a member of the Oklahoma Legislature. Interestingly, his father was a flute maker and craftsman. Courtesy of the Gray Major Collection.

Skyline Melodies

Another way to play something new is to focus on the surrounding landscape. Play high notes as the trees and mountains rise and low notes as the skyline drops. You can work your song all the way down to the ground. Everywhere you travel you are surrounded by music…you only need to look and play.

Triple Tonguing

One of the most advanced techniques that I am asked about is called Triple Tonguing. You can use Triple Tonguing at any point in a song; most artists use it near the front or back.

To perform this technique you'll need to say the word "took." Notice how your tongue moves in your mouth, the "T" just behind your teeth and the "K" toward the back of your hard pallet. Now try to say "took" with only your breath, no voice, about 20 times fast. If you're doing this correctly it should sound a bit like a runaway train. The final step is to place the flute to your lips and give it a try.

Advanced Play

So what makes an advanced player? Time is an obvious choice but not the answer I have in mind. I suppose the ability to play a wide range of notes is another good answer. I hear a lot of flute players who can play a lot of notes quickly – but that's still not what I have in mind.

An advanced player has the ability to emotionally move his or her audience with the flute. Many people can play a wide range of notes, can play quick flute runs, and have been playing for a long time but the flute sounds wooden (pardon the pun) and lifeless. An advanced player can play with an intensity that energizes an audience or brings them to tears. Think about the notes that you play and the amount of breath you place behind them. Think about what you want your audience to feel, or how you feel, when you play. A master flute player may choose to play a relatively simple arrangement of notes, but the effect of those notes can be very powerful.

I've been playing this instrument since the 1980s and am convinced that most of the notes I play were learned within the first 12 – 24 months. Everything from that point forward has been about my breath…not my ability to play dazzling combinations of notes.

Remember this: The Native Flute was first and foremost an instrument of passion and emotion. The flute's primary use was courtship – think seduction – and you want to speak volumes without speaking a single word. Do not let your ego get in the way of your song. Do not worry about how many songs you know or how many notes you can play. Do not worry about what is right and what is wrong…there is no right or wrong when playing the NAF. Just play.

"POP" Goes The End Of The Song

Native Flute songs will usually end in one of two ways. Either the last note will slowly fade off into the abyss or there will be a sudden blast of the final note. Most of the questions I get in my classes are about triple tonguing and the pop. If you have no idea what I'm referring to I suggest you listen to the CD now and them come back to the book. I've heard Clint Goss teach this technique and he tells his students to say "what" into the flute. "What" is the perfect word choice because the word mimics the sound you're trying to produce. Two things will determine your success with this technique…

1. You will need to considerably increase the amount of air pressure you're putting behind the note.

2. You will need to synchronize saying "what" with the last note played. Imagine that the "W" in "what" is said during the last second of the leading note. The rest of the word "what" – "hat," will happen as you're increasing your air pressure AND lifting your fingers from the flute. Try playing the pop by following the example below.

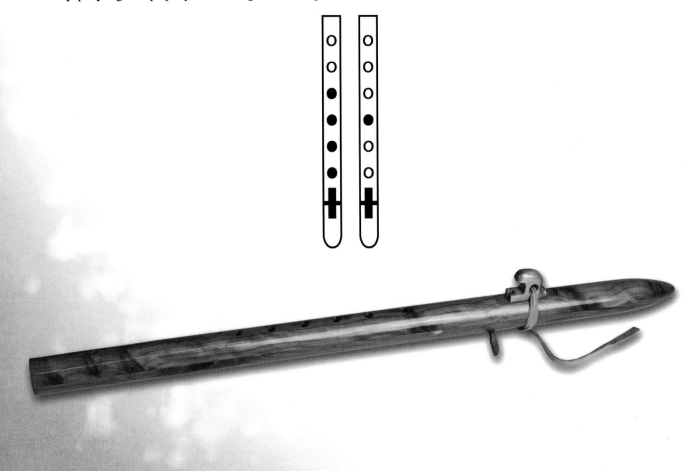

28

How To Choose The Best Flute For You

Selecting a flute is a very personal thing. The root note (lowest note on the flute) is what usually grabs you first. Work your way up the scale and see if you like how all the other notes sound and also how the flute feels in your hands. Are the holes too far apart for you? People with small or arthritic hands will probably be happy with a smaller – higher toned - flute so that reach won't be a problem. A flute tuned to A or B would probably be a good choice since the finger span will be the shortest.

Wood choice is something else to consider. Soft woods like cedar have a softer tone than hard woods like Ebony or Walnut. Many people feel that the hard woods sound too perfect and therefore they prefer softer woods like Cedar and Aspen.

If you intend to play your flute with other instruments, be aware of the maker's attention to tuning. While the flute may sound great by itself, it can sound just as bad when played with a piano or guitar.

Lastly, don't be drawn in by a beautifully carved flute that sounds horrible. Most of us have made this mistake and you probably will, too…but you've been warned.

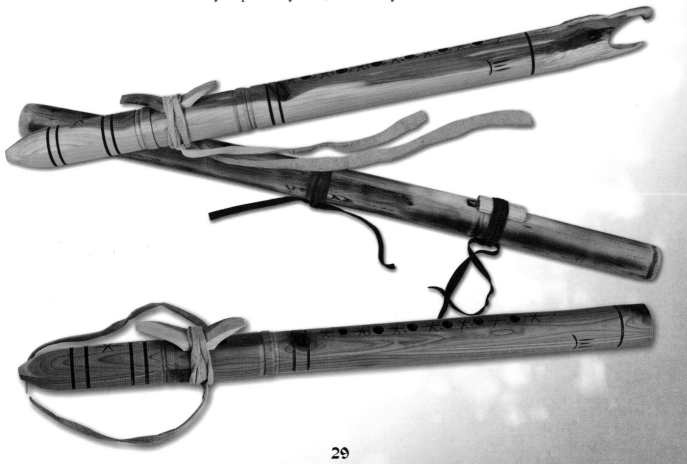

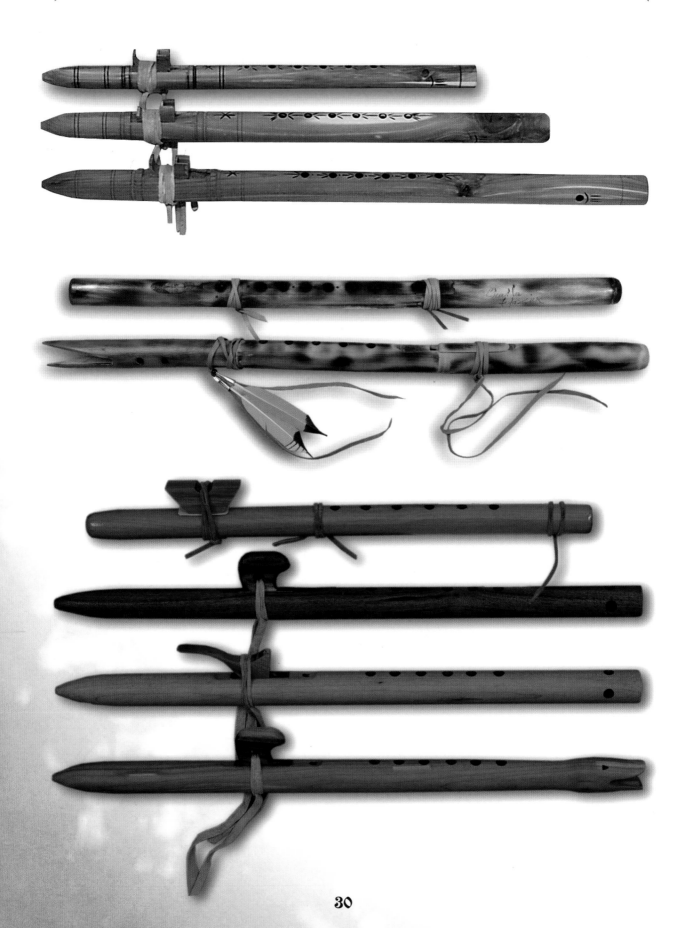

NAF Trouble Shooting

Q: *My flute won't do the over blow.*

A: Most Native American Style Flutes will play the over blow, but not all. If you are new to playing the flute, this can be seen as a blessing.

Q: *I can't play the root note without getting a horrible sounding squeak.*

A: You are either blowing too forcefully or you do not have all of the holes covered. Look in a mirror and find the gap.

Q: *My flute sounds great for a while and then the sound starts to cut out.*

A: There is probably too much moisture beneath the block. You will need to untie your block, shake the water out and dry the area beneath the block. You may want to use a hair band rather than the leather tie since it allows for a quick fix to this problem. As you advance, you'll probably experience this moisture build-up less. You will have this problem if you play outdoors in cold weather, too…be prepared and bring an extra flute or ten for cold weather play.

Q: *I was trying to play outside and the flute's voice would disappear every time the wind would blow.*

A: Try not to allow the wind to blow across your flute. I've played in some really strong winds and have great success when I turn my back to the wind OR turn into the wind.

Q: *My flute won't make any sound.*

A: Check the block and make certain that it's tightly secured and in it's proper place above the sound holes. Moving the block too far forward or back will cause the flutes note to be either sharp or flat. Neither is much of a problem unless you're playing with other instruments.

Q: *I was just told that my flute is not a Native American Flute because it was not made by an American Indian…what gives?*

A: There is no easy answer for this question as the subject is murky and subjective. All that I can tell you is, the design of the instrument you have is found only in North America. A lot of good people make flutes. A lot of American Indians make flutes. Sadly, there are also some shifty characters claiming to be Native making flutes and there must be a way to distinguish between the makers. Unless you enjoy conflict I advise you to play your flute as well as possible and leave the rest alone. Regardless of whether your flute was made by an American Indian or someone of another race, the design and notes "should be" almost indistinguishable…play on.

Q: *How can I learn more about the NAF once I finish with this book?*

A: A quick search of the Internet will lead you to a number of online resources. Clint Goss has a terrific web site called Flutopedia, which will tell you more than you ever imagined you could want to know about the NAF.

Q: *I still want to learn more about the NAF – where else can I go?*

A: Flute maker Geoffrey Ellis and I have created The Flute Portal and the grandfather of all NAF resources is INAFA (The International Native American Flute Association). The Flute Portal and INAFA will both lead you to Flute Circles, teachers, and flute events. INAFA hosts a NAF convention every other year that features concerts and workshops by the absolute top musicians in the field…don't miss it.

Q: *I've heard about Plains Flutes and Woodland Flutes, what's the difference?*

A: To the best of my understanding, the Woodlands voicing was a term created by Hawk Littlejohn to describe his flutes.

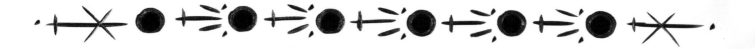

Song Writing Tips

It's great to know how to play a melody you've heard someone else play but even more rewarding to play your own. Getting started is the hard part but like most things it gets easier with time. Thankfully you've chosen to play an indigenous instrument and therefore classic songwriting structure doesn't have to apply. You can honestly play whatever your heart desires and it won't be wrong. Your song may not be pleasant and it's possible that nobody would want to listen, but it's not wrong. The freedom to play without concern for whether the melody is right or wrong allows many people to find their own voice…it did for me.

Here are a few basic tips to help you with your song writing. Although your melody doesn't have to conform to the traditional - it's probably what you know best and your audience is most accustomed to hearing.

1. Buy a recorder and have it running while you play. Most of what you record won't be used but you will get some things tracked that you're going to want to remember, but will forget, if you do not have a recorder tracking in the background. I cannot over state this point enough…always have the recorder tracking when you play!

2. Try writing a melody each day. It's not important to write a hit each day, only to make the habit of writing daily. It's also reasonable to write down any flute runs you come up with since they're good building blocks for future songs. Many of the solo tunes I write take several months to finish.

3. Don't worry if your song sounds a bit too much like another melody you have heard or wrote. Most songs have bits and pieces in common with other songs.

4. Use a prerecorded beat and freestyle over the beat. You'll be surprised at the melodies you stumble across when you are in the groove.

5. It's rare that all parts of your melody will fall into place and be perfect the first time. In fact, I am pretty sure that it's never happened for me on a solo flute song. More than likely you will have a good verse recorded during one session and the chorus will have been tracked at another time. You just need to figure out which parts go together making the song you want to play.

6. Once you have assembled the basic structure of your song it is a good idea to play it through several times while the recorder is going so you can step back and hear it whether or not the tune needs to be revised. You will know when it's a finished piece.

7. When playing with other instruments, resist the urge to play over the entire song. The longer I play the more I appreciate silence and the space between my notes.

8. Everyone hits a wall from time to time. Do not try to force your tune… let it happen. You may need to step away from a tune for a while and revisit it when your mind is in a different place.

Practice Song #1 - Amazing Grace

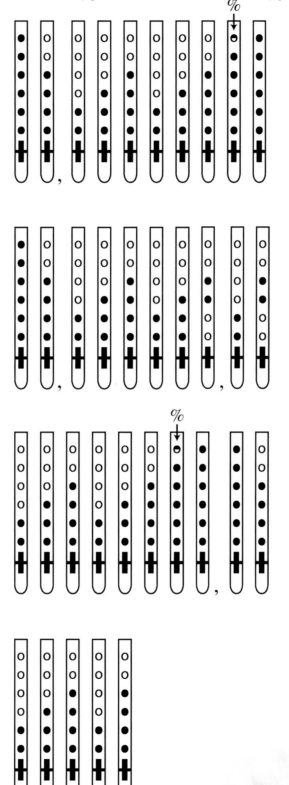

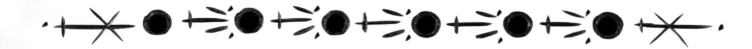

Practice Song #2 - Never Alone

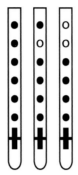 Repeat 2x

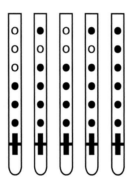

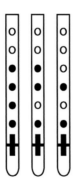 Repeat 2x

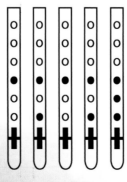

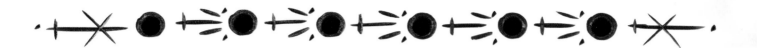

Short Hand

When I first began working with the flute and wanted to keep track of my ideas I'd sit and draw a bunch of flutes, coloring the holes as I go. This was a tedious process and eventually led me to create a master sheet of blank flute drawings. The master sheet worked well enough until my guitarist Sennen Quigley had a better idea. He suggested the following…

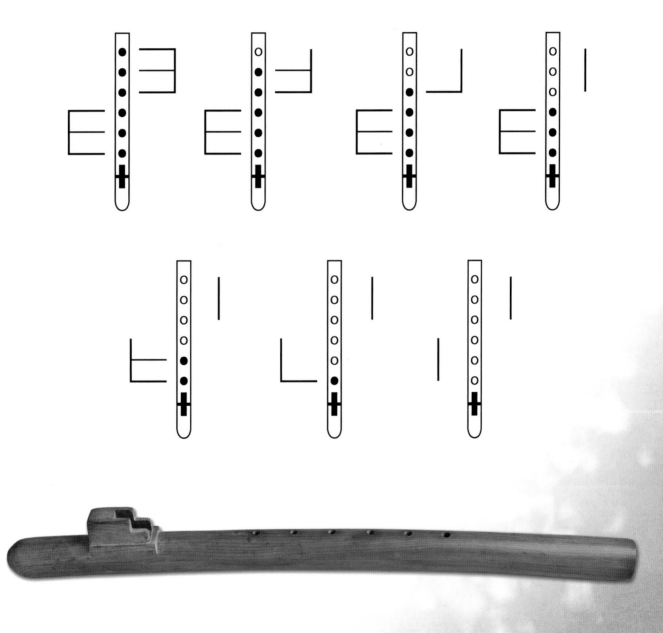

37

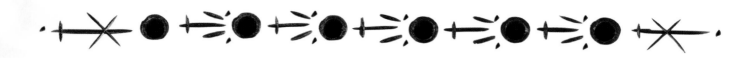

Blank Composition Sheet

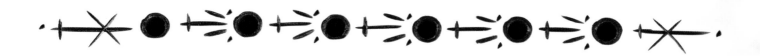

Blank Composition Sheet

Conclusion

I've been playing the Native Flute for decades and I'm still learning. I hope that you have found the lessons in this manual helpful and a good starting point for your journey with the flute. I highly suggest that you listen to as many flute players as possible, present day and archival recordings too. Develop an ear for the phrasing used with the NAF and learn to develop your own style rather than simply trying to play like your favorite artist. The lessons included here are few in number but should cover just about everything you will need to know. There is nothing here that you would not have stumbled across on your own... hopefully I've sped up the process.

The first version of this manual was titled *Trailhead of the American Indian Courting Flute*. *Native American Courting Flute* not only covers a lot of the same material but goes beyond the lessons of the original. Many of the topics covered here were inspired by the workshops I've taught.

It has been my pleasure to help get you started with the flute and I sincerely hope that if we're ever in the same place you'll be kind enough to share your experiences with me.

Courting scene by Doc Tate Nevaquaya, Comanche. Courtesy of the Gray Major Collection.